ARCHITECTURAL
Self-Guided
TOURS

by
MARSHA CUDWORTH

Lady Raspberry Press

New York, N.Y.
1997

Library of Congress catalog #84-081044
First Edition
First Printing 1985
Second Printing 1987
Third Printing 1989
Fourth Printing 1993
Revised Fifth Printing 1997
ISBN #0-9608554-2-4

Cover Photo: The Joseph Hall House
    Walking Tour, Loop A Site #28
Back Cover Photo: The Mainstay Inn
    Walking Tour, Loop A Site #3
Cover Photographs, Book Design and Production
    by Howard Michaels

Photo-Graphics® by Howard Michaels
Pen and Ink Artwork by Marsha Cudworth
Charles Wissman, Graphics and Technical Consultant
Historic American Buildings Survey (HABS) drawings by
    Cape May Survey Teams of 1973, 1974, 1977.
Printed in China

The Photo-Graphics® appearing in this publication are a collaboration of efforts. The striking illustrations are achieved by an original combination of high contrast photo techniques with additional details drawn in with pen and ink.

Bathing Scene near the Pier

Table of Contents

CAPE ISLAND
The Cape May of Yesteryear
Reprinted from Victorian Holidays (Lady Raspberry Press, 1982)

There are many seaside resort towns in the United States today, but few can compare with the rich historical background of Cape May, New Jersey. An understanding of its phenomenal rediscovery must begin with an appreciation of its past.

Early records indicate that a band of peace loving Lenni-Lenape Indians sought relief from the summer heat on Cape Island's shores, and were there when the first white men sailed their ships along the coast and into the bay.

In 1620, the same year the Pilgrims landed on Plymouth Rock, Captain Cornelius Jacobsen Mey explored New Jersey and the Delaware Bay area. He declared the climate of these fruitful lands as good as his homeland of Holland and named Cape May for himself.

Many of the first settlers were whalers from New England and it has been reputed that more descendants of the Mayflower Pilgrims lived in Cape May than anywhere else!

`Its ensuing popularity as a resort may have begun as early as 1766 when Robert Parsons placed an advertisement in the *Pennsylvania Gazette*, offering for sale his 254 acre plantation situated one mile from the resort of Cape May, "which would be very convenient for taking in such people (tourists)". However, it was not until the early 1800's that visitors would be drawn in great numbers from Philadelphia, as well as from

other cities in Pennsylvania, Delaware and Maryland. Cape May was also a great attraction for rich plantation owners and other members of "Southern Society". Interestingly, the Cape was considered part of the South and actually fell below a projected Mason-Dixon line.

The earliest travelers form Philadelphia came by stagecoach and took as long as two days to traverse the sandy roads of South Jersey. Others came by sailing sloops, steamboats and packet boats. By the mid-1800's, steamboat lines offered a daily run from Philadelphia to Cape May for $6 round trip including meals. Steamtrains soon took care of the overland journey and carried passengers from Philadelphia and points further south by way of Baltimore.

Right from the start, there seemed to be an abundance of visitors and a shortage of accommodations. Private boarding houses soon gave way to licensed "public houses" which were little more than barn-like dormitories, partitioned with curtains for sleeping: men on one side, women on the other.

The segregation of ladies and gentlemen also extended to their swimming hours: a red flag signaled the men to the water; a white flag, the ladies. Bathers of this era wore an abundance of clothing into the ocean—tunics, pants, skirts, white collars and wristbands, stockings, bathing shoes and even straw hats! All this for "modesty's sake" and to avoid the sun. Tanned skin was an indication of the labor class who had to work outside during daytime hours.

During the midday heat, guests withdrew to the public rooms of their establishments—to the dining areas, game rooms, the card room, the writing room, the lobby, and to the most favorite spot of all—the veranda, where society could see and be seen. Clothes were of the utmost importance and were changed several times a day. Men wore three-piece suits, top hats and carried canes. The women dressed in voluminous skirts (with waist-clinching corsets underneath) and carried parasols to protect their alabaster complexions.

Members of this fashionable elite strolled along the avenues or went for carriage rides on the hard packed sand. While ladies played ten-pin or cooled themselves on the open verandas, the men gambled in clubs, sharpened their skills in shooting galleries, or bet on horse races on the beach.

Cape May of the mid-nineteenth century saw a procession of presidents and statesmen visiting the resort—Franklin Pierce being the first president, followed by Chester A. Arthur and Ulysses S. Grant. Senator Henry Clay came in 1847 seeking solace following the death of his son. Twelve years before he was to become president, Congressman Abraham Lincoln, on a Whig campaign tour, may have checked into the Mansion House with his wife. (The signature of "A. Lincoln" found on a guest register there, has caused great dispute of its true identity!). Cape May also saw the likes of John Phillip Sousa, as he played a newly-composed march called "Congress Hall" on the lawn of that famous hotel which still stands today. The list of dignitaries grew with visits from Empress Carlotta, British actress Lily Langtry, writer Bret Harte and Clara Barton.

The golden age of grandeur reached ultimate heights with the heralded opening of The Mount Vernon, billed in the *Illustrated London News* on September 17, 1853, as a "palatial building far exceeding any hotel in England." When completed, it would accommodate 3,500 guests and hold place-settings for 2,500. The four-story hotel had miles of balconies and verandas that wrapped around its exterior and was entirely lit by gas manufactured on its premises. On September 5, 1856, with only the final wing to be completed, the grand structure was found to be on fire. Within an hour and a half, it had burned to the ground.

Understandably, with prevailing high winds and little fire-fighting equipment on hand, blazes led to disastrous results, often destroying large sections of the town. The largest of these, in 1878, took with it the entire hotel district and substantially reduced the town's capacity to accommodate the vast number of visitors to Cape May. Although unfortunate, the fires provided fresh opportunities for new construction. During the 1860's, 70's, and 80's, hundreds of buildings were fabricated in every major architectural style of the Victorian era.

Contributing to this building boom were the wealthy Philadelphia "Main Liners", the owners of the excursion steamboats and railroads, rich merchants, bankers and the like, who were all displeased with overflowing hotels and crowds. They secured the best architects, builders and carpenters and commissioned them to create private summer residences—as large and as fashionable as money could buy! These new wooden structures exuberantly competed with each other for the most lavish ornamentation—latticework, scrolls and frets, brackets and bargeboards. Each architectural detail was painted a different color, to accentuate the skillful craftsmanship.

During the summers of 1890-91, President Benjamin Harrison and his wife spent much time in a private cottage at Cape May Point, owned by his Postmaster General, John Wanamaker (the Philadelphia department store magnate). Wanamaker was one of the founders of Cape May Point. The President set up his working headquarters in Congress Hall (which was the resort's most famous hotel of that time), thus establishing the Summer White House concept.

At the turn of the century (1903), crowds of 20,000 waited all week to witness Henry Ford's beach skimmer compete with the world's top race car drivers in a week-long racing event.

Fires continued sporadically and the town still had no appreciable fire-fighting equipment. Tourists grew apprehensive as they were packed into overflowing wooden hotels. Soon, newly installed train lines and the advent of the automobile lured society to vacation at some of the more modern resorts, such as Atlantic City, further north. Cape May's golden age declined, with a brief revival during Prohibition with its bootlegging and rum-running. Following the roar of the 20's, the seaside town evolved into another sleepy South Jersey community with the yet unrecognized distinction of having the greatest collection of late 19th century buildings in the United States today.

INTRODUCTION TO THE SELF-GUIDED TOURS

This handbook is intended for all visitors to Cape May, serving as an illustrated guide to its rich architectural heritage and varied points of interest.

In 1976, the entire town of Cape May was designated a National Historic Landmark with a collection of over 600 late 19th century frame structures, many of which are individually listed on the National Register of Historic Places.

Cape May offers its visitors countless opportunities for exploration, with an atmosphere that might have been brushed in by an artist of the 1800's – one hundred year old streets lined with majestic shade trees and fascinating Victorian architecture; gazebos and gardens splashed with colorful blooms of hydrangea, impatiens and tiger-lilies, a charming beach edged with jaunty bright tents and an oceanfront promenade stretching from sunrise to sunset!

Turn almost any corner in this seashore village and you catch a glimpse of our heritage from another century. An attentive eye will discover and delight in a richness of handcrafted detail that is rarely seen today. This is, for example, a town of porches–porches in every conceivable variation. Whenever possible, the Victorians built their porches so that they could view the sea. If not blessed with an ocean view, they did the next best thing–they built their porches so as to get a good glimpse of one another! This is the sort of detail we are examining–the charms of another era which still permeate this community and still contribute certain amenities that are unlikely to be duplicated today.

Suggestions for Using the Guide:

The Self-Guided Walking Tours are laid out in two separate Loops to allow you to explore the town leisurely. Allow yourself approximately 1-1/2 hours for each walking tour and about 2 hours for the auto tour, which may include several "rest and/or explore" stops and a sunset viewing.

- Pick an early to mid-morning or late afternoon/early evening to do the walking tours at the height of the summer season. During the spring, fall and winter, anytime is splendid for the tour!

- First, familiarize yourself with the points of interest and their location on the Site-Guide Street Map. You might browse through the Guide before walking through the tour, or take a bike ride about–just let your eyes wander and delight in the sights!

- When ready to take the tour, put on a pair of comfortable walking shoes, take this guide with you and proceed to one of the starting points (see map) and be prepared for an enjoyable trip back in time.

- Loop 1 leads you through a relatively all-residential section of the town–you'll pass by several historic hotels, a number of restored bed & breakfast inns and many private residences on quiet tree-lined streets.

- Loop II brings you past a wide variety of structure–historic hotels, bed & breakfast inns, private residences, and a number of commercial shops and eateries for those who may want to include shopping or a meal during their tour.

- The Auto Tour will give you an overall view of the city layout from one end of town to the other, and includes a ride to the historic Lighthouse and State Park at Cape May Point. This tour can also be a delightful day bike-trip for the experienced biker.

- As you use this guide, you will notice that many of the sites have been artfully photographed and illustrated for easier identification. Each individual site being viewed has a number which corresponds to its location on the Site Guide Street Map.

- For your general use, we have included a handy Glossary of Architectural Terms and an illustrated Architectural Construction Composite which identifies the most commonly referred to parts of a 19th century structure.

- This newest edition includes a Street Level Guide featuring descriptions and illustrations of all major architectural styles found in Cape May.

- When reading the description of each site, note that the historical title for each house is set in italics and the present-day name for the structure is set in bold face type.

- All directions for the walking and auto tours are set in italics and correspond to the shaded path areas on all street maps.

Glossary of Architectural Terms

The following definitions which refer to the most common 19th century architectural terms have been adapted and derived from The American Glossary of Architectural Terms, George O. Garnsey, author, Chicago, IL: National Builder Publishing Co., 1887.

Acroterium - a symmetrical ornamentation usually placed at the apex of a roof.

Arcade - a series of arches, supported on columns or pilasters.

Baluster - a small column or post, supporting a hand rail.

Balustrade - a collection or series of balusters supporting a hand rail; all the balusters comprising the railing system.

Bargeboards - a decorated board used to finish off a gable, covering the ends of the rafters (also called vergeboard).

Beltcourse - a collection of moldings or flat projecting facings attached horizontally to the wall.

Belvedere - a high turret; a lookout pavilion located at the rooftop.

Board and Batten - a type of siding involving a combination of vertical boards covered by narrow moldings at the joining point.

Bracket - an ornamental brace or support fixed against a vertical surface, supporting weight.

Bric-a-brac - a common phrase for the assortment of curiosities and works of art used for decoration or embellishment.

Captain's Walk - common term used for a small, often elaborate, rooftop structure used for ocean viewing.

Clapboard - a thin board used as a covering to the walls of a frame building.

Column - a perpendicular pillar used to support weight or part of a building.

Corbel - a structural projection built into a wall and projecting from its face.

Cornice Bracket - an ornamental molding which is part of the support system in the roof overhang.

Cresting - rooftop ornamentation.

Cupola - a small vault or dome rising in a circular or elliptical curve from the top of an edifice.

Dado - the portion of the wall of a room above the baseboard and below the next collection of moldings. Also, the solid, plain portion of a classic pedestal.

Dormer - a window set into a small projecting gable in the attic or roof area of the structure.

Eaves - the overhang of a roof which projects past the edge.

Eyebrow Dormer - a low dormer set in an arched roofline having the contours of the outline of an eyebrow.

Facade - the front or elevation of a building.

Fanlight - a transom light; a fan-like window set over a doorway.

Finial - the vertical finishing ornament to any architectural design.

Fish Scale Shingles - wooden shingles with curved bottom edges, resembling the scales of a fish.

Fluting - semi-circular cavities as in a classic column.

Foliated - decorations or carvings arranged in a leaf motif.

Fretwork - ornamentally patterned and carved woodwork.

Gable - a common roof type where the enclosed end of a pitched roof forms a triangle.

Gazebo - a small outdoor structure, usually displaying fancy embellishments.

Gingerbread Style - Refers to the American counterpart of Victorian-style architecture characterized by fanciful carpentry and ornamentation. Popular during reign of Queen Victoria (1837-1901).

Gothic Arch - an arch with a pointed apex.

Hood Molding - a molding generally placed over a window or doorway for the purpose of throwing off the rain.

Keystone - a wedge-shaped stone found at the center of an arch.

Lattice - the interlacing and crossing of wood or metal so as to form a geometrical pattern.

Mansard Roof - a steep, hipped roof on all four sides, finished as an attic or upper story. Named for its inventor, Francoise Mansard (1598-1666), it became popular during Victorian times for it provided a full floor of tax-exempt living space above the roof line, as the law taxed only the number of floors *below* the roofline.

Molding - an architectural detail giving a projecting contour or outline to a surface.

Palladium Window - square-headed windows flanking the sides of an arched opening or window.

Pediment - the gable or triangular portion of a classic cornice.

Pendant - an ornamental post usually hanging from the peak of a Gothic-style roof, forming the starting of the truss.

Pergola - an arbor or shaded walk, often latticed above stone pillars or wooden posts.

Portico - a covered walkway, open on at least one side, and supported by a row of columns or pillars.

Quatrefoil - a Gothic ornamental form derived by the arrangement of four intersecting circles; a circular form divided into four leaf-like sections.

Quoin - the blocks of stone generally used to decorate and finish the external angle of a building.

Relief - carvings that project from the surface.

Rib - a molding projection dividing a Gothic vault, roof or ceiling.

Spandril - a triangular space or panel between the outer curve of an arch and the square framework enclosing it.

Steeple - the tower or spire of a church; any lofty erection of a conical or pointed shape.

Terra-Cotta - burned or baked clay pieces, molded and often used for roof tiles and ornamentation.

Tracery - small radiating pattern work subdividing windows and panels.

Transom - a frame or bar across a window; a window opening above a doorway.

Trellis - a screen or latticework used to support climbing plants.

Turret - a small pinnacle or tower at the corner of a wall.

Vault - an arched roof of masonry.

Veranda - an open porch with a roof.

Vergeboard - an often richly ornamented board placed along the slant of the gable roof to conceal the end of the rafters.

Vestibule - the first room at the entrance of a house.

Victorian - refers to the revival of 19th century-style architecture popular in England during the reign of Queen Victoria (1837-1901). Also refers to the corresponding American adaptations.

Widow's Walk - a small platform at the top of a roof, nicknamed as such for the women who stood there and gazed out to sea in search of their seafaring husbands.

Major Structural Details of Cape May Architecture

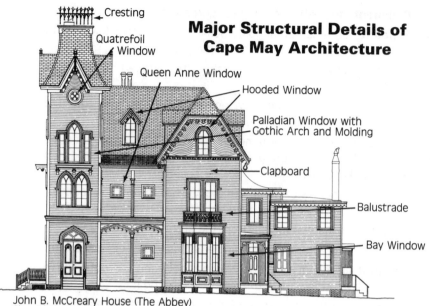

Cresting

Quatrefoil Window

Queen Anne Window

Hooded Window

Palladian Window with Gothic Arch and Molding

Clapboard

Balustrade

Bay Window

John B. McCreary House (The Abbey)
Site #8 Walking Tour, Loop A

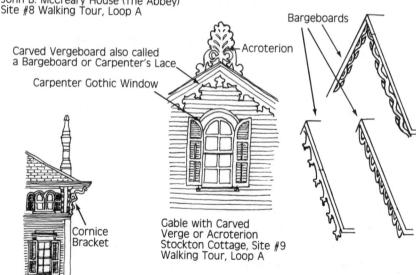

Carved Vergeboard also called a Bargeboard or Carpenter's Lace

Carpenter Gothic Window

Acroterion

Bargeboards

Gable with Carved Verge or Acroterion
Stockton Cottage, Site #9
Walking Tour, Loop A

Cornice Bracket

American Bracketed Villa Detail, George Allen House, Site #6, Auto Tour, Loop A

Wrought Iron Fencing Designs

211 Congress Place

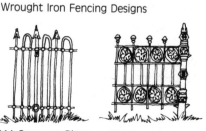

515 Franklin Street

Hipped Roof

Mansard Roof

Flat Roof
with Parapet

Gabled Roof

Gambrel Roof

Finial

Fretwork

Pendant

Board and
Batten

Gable with Carved Verge
and Finial
Pink House, Site #42,
Walking Tour, Loop B

Cut Wood Shingles

Fishscale Shingles

Timbering (Stick Style)

Column

Carved Wood Spandrel
Arch Pink House, Site #42,
Walking Tour, Loop B

Ornamental Brick Chimney
Physick House, Site #10,
Auto Tour, Loop A

645 Hughes Street
Site #28 Walking Tour,
Loop A

621 Lafayette Street

653 Washington Street
Site #3, Auto Tour, Loop A

Cottages on Columbia Avenue

ARCHITECTURAL STYLES OF THE 19TH AND EARLY 20TH CENTURIES
A Street-Level Guide to Cape May's Houses

On the streets of Cape May stand the examples of a period of great architectural vitality. The architects and carpenters of the 19th century produced an enduring variety of buildings which freely reflected foreign styles and historical periods. American architecture of this time was influenced by popular styles particularly in Great Britain, France, Italy and adapted these to our own local needs, climate and availability of building materials. Of equal importance, the 1896 Centennial Exposition in Philadelphia exposed Americans to Oriental architecture for the first time.

The reoccurrence of Oriental stimuli at subsequent expositions influenced American architecture by bringing such basic, yet enduring, design qualities as the open house plan, latticework, extended eaves, a craftsman-like assembly of parts and the integration of a building with its landscaped setting, to the American architectural scene.

All of these foreign and historical influences are described in the following major architectural styles found in Cape May, New Jersey. Although of rather conservative nature, the classic 19th century examples still standing in Cape May today, reflect an outstanding variety and exuberance.

Gothic Revival (ca. 1840-1880)

The Gothic Revival style from England was the earliest of the "romantic" revival styles from Europe to influence house design in this country. The American version was loosely based on elements of medieval architecture borrowing on richly picturesque decorative tracery, towers, pointed windows, trefoils and parapets. This charming "fairy tale" cottage style became popular among middle-class homeowners who could afford a builder but not an architect. The timely invention of the jigsaw permitted an endless variety of decorative wooden carving often called "gingerbread". These "Carpenter Gothic" cottages featured in newly-available pattern books, providing the public with floor plans and building specifications. A Gothic Revival house is usually of two-story height, steeply pitched roof with one or more front-facing gables typically outlined with carved vergeboard. Delicately decorated porches, bay windows and dormers are common. Vertical proportions are obvious and general richness is enhanced by use of multi-color earth tones. *(See Sites No. 7, 8, 31, 41.)*

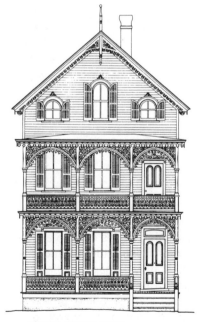

Eldridge Johnson House

Stockton Cottage   (HABS)

Italianate (ca. 1840-1875)

As the most expansive of the Victorian styles, Italianate houses are common in both urban and rural areas of this country. The Italian prototypes (Italian palaces of 16th and 17th centuries and Italian farmhouses) inspired two distinctly American building styles appearing in Cape May–the Renaissance Revival (1840-1920) and the American Bracketed Villa (1840-1880). Both hybrid American styles have architectural and decorative elements borrowed from the Italianate: shallow hip roof, overhanging eaves with ornate supporting brackets and arched windows with decorative window hoods. Larger versions can have towers, roof cupolas and large columned verandas. There are no purely Italianate examples in Cape May. (See Renaissance Revival and American Bracketed Villa.)

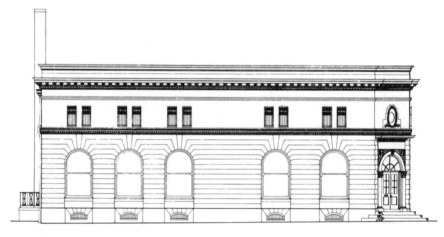

New Jersey Trust & Safe Deposit Co. (McDowell's Gallery) (HABS)

Renaissance Revival (ca. 1840-1920)

An American style derived from Italianate palaces of 16th and 17th centuries and often used for commercial structures in more urban areas. Buildings display a formal, stately elegance defined by symmetry, ornamentation and building materials. Characteristics include a very low, almost hidden roofline, prominent cornice brackets; each story clearly defined by a decorative belt course; windows varying in size form story to story; and an arcaded and stoneworked ground floor. *(See Sites No. 53, Auto Tour No. 1.)*

American Bracketed Villa (ca. 1863-1890)

Distinctly American, this suburban style derives decorative elements from the Italian villa and farmhouse styles. Well suited for ocean-side living, these structures, with double-doorways and floor to ceiling walk-through windows leading to open verandas, well extend the living space to the outdoors. General characteristics include a square or rectangular shape, symmetrical facade, low-pitched hip roof, cupola, large chimneys with molded terra-cotta chimney pots, overhanging eaves with large supportive carved brackets and large windows with shutters. (See Sites No. 1, 3, 45, 46, 49, 56; Auto Tour No. 6.)

The Page House (The Bedford)   *Barry Marron*

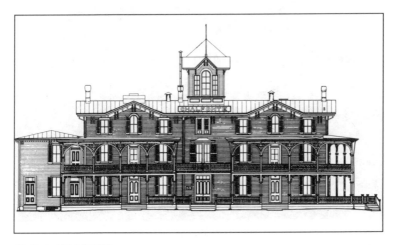

Chalfonte Hotel (HABS)

Second Empire (ca. 1850-1890)
(also called Mansard Style)

The most distinguishing feature is the tall Mansard roof which provides a full story at the attic level. (In France, this was popular because it gave its owners a full story of tax-free living since they were taxed on property *below* the roof line!) This style is the result of an era when Paris was considered the most fashionable and modern city in the world. Popularized grand architecture built in France's Second Empire under Napoleon III, had great impact on American design and Cape May has dozens of these structures illustrating the variety and adaptability of this style. Additional characteristics include a tall, boldly modeled, three-dimensional style with paneled freeze-boards, a symmetrical facade, dormer windows, multi-color slate roof and cast iron roof cresting. Like the Italianate style, Second Empire houses have bracketed eaves, cornices, bold arched window hoods and ornate verandas. Often enlivened with rich and colorful paint schemes, this style produced some of the most decorative Victorian houses - the classic image of the "Victorian mansion". *(See sites No. 11, 12, 43, 55.)*

The Douglas Gregory House. (The Queen Victoria)   *Don McDonough*

Emlen Physick House (Emlen Physick Estate Museum) (HABS)

Stick (ca. 1840-1890)

The 1876 Centennial Exposition in Philadelphia exposed Americans to Oriental architecture for the first time. Subsequent appearances of Japanese architecture in illustrated books, the 1893 Columbian Exposition in Chicago and a Japanese village erected in San Francisco's Exposition of 1894, influenced and gave new direction to the design of the American house. Aided by pattern books, popular views of Andrew Jackson Downing (architectural theorist) and American architects predisposed to the Japanese constructivist esthetic, a skeletal Stick-style emerged. The most notable characteristic is the use of structural framing materials for exterior ornament. Stick-style details are comprised of raised wooden boards placed over the siding to simulate the skeleton of the building. Steeply pitched gable roofs with overhanging eaves, have decorative trusses, while porch columns are supported by diagonal braces. The Stick-style was made popular by British architect Gervase Wheeler who came to this country in the 1840's. His book, *Rural Home* (1851) became very popular and was influential in promoting the Stick style for residential architecture. *(See Site No. 52, Auto Tour No. 10, 43.)*

Queen Anne (ca. 1876-1910)

The Queen Anne style was brought from Queen Victoria's England and introduced to America at the Philadelphia Centennial Exposition in 1876. As the last of the Victorian styles, its hallmark is its eclecticism, embodying the Victorian love of variety, industry and excess. The informality of the Queen Anne style suggested the wholesome countryside. Factories mass-producing countless decorative building details during the 1880's encouraged the use of many materials appearing on the same facade: brick, stone, clapboarding, shingles and half-timbering. Despite its variety, the style has several typical elements: an asymmetrical front facade with doorway to one side, complex and steep multi-gabled roof, prominent bay window and single-story porches. Structural details include turrets, iron roof cresting, massive stone chimneys, dormers, turned wooden rail posts and stained glass panels in window uppers. *(See Sites No. 15, 23, 35, 47, 54,60.)*

Dr. Henry F. Hunt House
(HABS)

I. Leaming Sheppard House (The Prince Edward)
(Ken Frye)

Romanesque Revival (ca. 1840-1900)

Another European style architecture (European Romanesque, 1000-1200) which was introduced into this country in the 1840's developed into three distinct categories: Romanesque Revival (ca. 1840-1900), Victorian Romanesque (1870-1890) and Richardsonian Romanesque (1870-1900). The expansive and creative use of masonry made these structures costly to build. Richardsonian Revival homes were popular among successful "robber barons" of the period and Romanesque Revival examples were almost exclusively built as churches and public buildings. General characteristics feature gabled or hipped roof; symmetrical or asymmetrical facade; towers; vertical silhouette; fortress-like appearance; squared stonework; deeply recessed windows and doors with semi-circular arch; hood-molding over windows; compound arches at every portal and arcaded corbels under eaves and at belt courses. *(See Site Auto Tour No. 2.)*

M. Cudworth

St. Mary's Roman Catholic Church (Our Lady of the Sea)

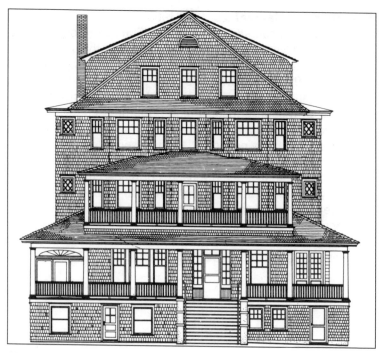

Macomber Hotel (HABS)

Shingle (ca. 1880-1900)

Early Shingle-style homes were built by architects as large summer cottages for the wealthy in the seaside resorts of Rhode Island and Massachusetts. Combining elements of Colonial and Queen Anne styles, the Shingle house has a uniquely American look and appealed to the late-Victorian interest in the natural landscape. (Turn of the century architects and social theorists of the time saw the suburban lifestyle just a short step away from "utopian wilderness".) Simple facades, devoid of applied ornamentation, natural wood treatment and extensive open porch areas gave this style an organized look. Structural details may include squat towers, large stone porch supports, projecting bays, dormer windows and strips of multi-paned windows. Cape May's examples include both Shingle-style and Shingled-Dutch Colonial Revival style which featured a gambrel roof. *(See Site 21; Auto Tour No. 14, 25.)*

Bungalow (ca. 1890-1940)

Very popular in this country between 1900 and 1920, the basic Bungalow inspired the creation of practical and affordable homes that were economical to build and easy to maintain. (One could buy the entire makeup of a Bungalow home for as little as $393.00 from the Sears catalog!) Cobblestone, fieldstone and shingle treatments were used to give the Bungalow a rustic hand-crafted look. The Bungalow-style building originated in British India as a one-story pavilion surrounded by verandas and used as way stations for travelers. The name was derived from the Hindi word *bangla*, meaning "native dwelling" and coined by the British to describe the hot weather homes built by themselves on the subcontinent. Typical Bungalow houses are square, small, single-story with a gently sloping gable roof that extends from house to porch. Overhanging eaves protecting against the sun, expose roof beams and rafters; clustered porch columns rise from sloping stone or shingled piers which support the front porch roof. Dormered windows are shed style or low pitched gable. The sole ornamentation may be decoratively paneled double-hung windows. *(See Site No. 26.)*

Bell Bungalow   M. Cudworth

Wilmon Wildin
Florida Cottage
(HABS)

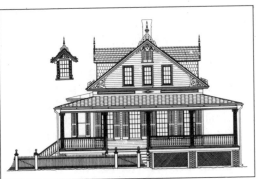

Period Revivals (1870-1940)

Note: *Architectural revivals during this period were, in part, a reaction against the eclecticism of the preceding period. The popularity of the Centennial Exposition of 1876 exposed people to America's 18th century heritage and the styles of the English, Dutch and Spanish were studied and imitated, as well as the Federal style of the early Republic. The following three styles have examples in Cape May.*

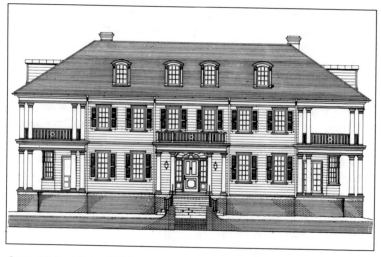

George W. Boyd House (HABS)

Georgian Revival (ca. 1870-1920)

Original Georgian homes in this country were built by wealthy residents of Eastern trading towns to replace their simple, early wooden structures. (The name *Georgian* refers to English kings in power from 1714-1830.) The style was inspired by Roman classicism and the later Georgian Revival Style also displays original building materials and methods of the formal, symmetrical and heavily detailed classic style house. General characteristics show a rectangular and symmetrical shape., a hip or gambrel roof, columns, pilasters, pediments over doors and windows and decorative moldings defining the facade. The prominent central doorway is frequently topped by Palladian window. Northern houses are usually built of clapboard with a central chimney; Southern examples are brick with paired end chimneys. Formal Georgian houses have balustrades or a widow's walk decorating a hipped roof. *(See Sites Auto Tour No. 15, 18.)*

Spanish Colonial Revival (ca. 1915-1940)

After World War I, the Spanish Colonial Revival style flourished in suburbs nationwide due to a resurgent interest in historical styles and the connection it had to a relaxed Southwestern warm-weather environment. This style was especially popular in planned suburbs of California and the Southwest as well as a sprinkling of resort towns up and down the East Coast. Most notable characteristics of the Spanish Colonial Revival Style are the plain exterior walls of stucco (imitating the adobe of the early Spanish colonial missions) and the low pitched red tile roof with arched doors and windows. Entry doors may be double paneled and ornamented with carving, spiral columns or pilasters; triple-arched window arcades with wood or iron grillwork and fancy chimney tops. Other details include projecting eaves, rafters and water spouts, small balconies and towers. Expanded versions of the house may extend horizontally or vertically with an arched open-sided gallery lined with pillars or a Mission-style facade. *(See Sites No. 6, Auto Tour No. 20.)*

Nelson Z. Graves House (The Mission Inn)   *Edith Hewitt*

Cape Island Baptist Church   *H. Michaels*

Josiah Schellinger House (The Octagonal House) M. Cudworth

Exotic Revival (ca. 1830-1890)

Influenced by Egyptian, Moorish and Octagon Styles, these revivals became known to Americans through French and British expeditions in the East. (French invasion of Egypt and British colonization of the Middle East generated great interest in all things Oriental.) The use of Islamic or Moorish details on buildings of any style was quite common *(See Site No. 51).* A large number of Octagon-style homes were built around the time of the Civil War. The style originated with the publication of the 1848 book, A Home for All, or the Gravel Wall and Octagon Mode of Building by Orson Squire Fowler. Fowler, a phrenologist and marriage counselor, advocated many modern improvements to the domestic home: hot and cold running water, indoor flush toilets and filtered drinking water. His Octagonal style boasted more space than a square house, more light, easier to heat and cool. The Octagonal style also often appeared in the form of Victorian park and garden architecture, gazebo and belvedere structures and botanical conservatories. *(See Site Auto Tour No. 57, 58.)*

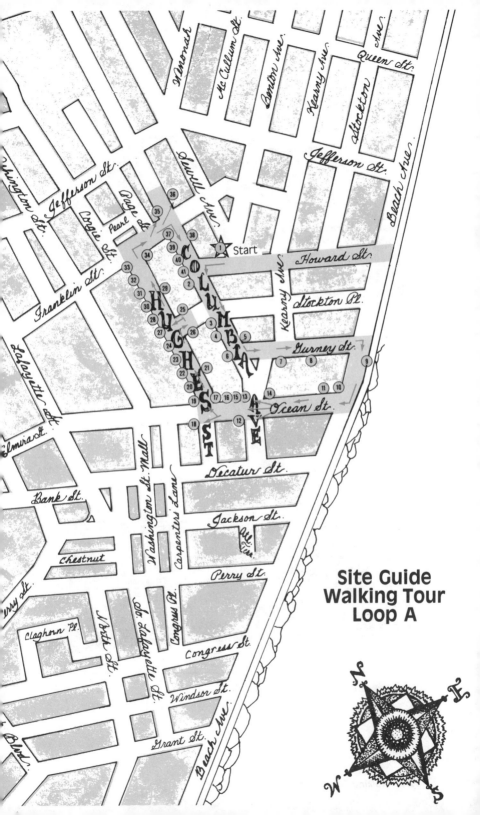

Site Guide
Walking Tour
Loop A

The Chalfonte Hotel   1878 Letterhead

John Tack residence (The Victorian Rose).   *M. Cudworth*

WALKING TOUR
LOOP A: SITES 1-41

1. Corner of Howard Street and Sewell Avenue, **The Chalfonte Hotel**, 1875: Erected for Henry Sawyer, Cape May's Civil War hero and the object of a prisoner exchange for the son of General Robert E. Lee. This is an American Bracketed Villa with Italianate decorative elements–notice the belvedere or cupola topping the roof and the large veranda. Owned by the Satterfield family since 1911, the Chalfonte today is owned and operated by two teachers with the help of a large hotel staff. The public volunteers its help with the enormous maintenance job by attending off-season "work-weekends" in the spring and fall. The Chalfonte is Cape May's oldest operating hotel. The light of a very early morning sun provides a stunning view of the two-story colonnaded wing on the Sewell Avenue side of the building. Dining room and King Edward Bar open to the public. Seasonal.

Turn left at Columbia for a sampling of this Avenue's charming cottages. Straight ahead at intersection view:

2. 715 Columbia Avenue, *John Tack residence,* 1872-73 **(The Victorian Rose)**: Designed by Stephen Decatur Button (Cape May's most prolific architect), showing traces of the pointed or Gothic style. Notice the intricate wood bric-a-brac, the repeating arches and pillars, the wraparound porch and a summer Victorian rose garden. The two houses next door, 719 (The Brass Bed) and 725 (Linda Lee Bed & Breakfast), were also designed by S. D. Button. Check tour #40 and #41 for similarities. Bed and Breakfast Inn. Christmas Tour. Open all year.

Continue south along Columbia Avenue noting typical Victorian structures and the variety of carpenter's trim.

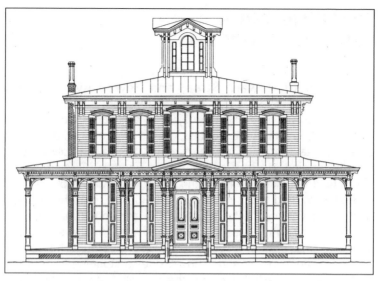

Jackson's Clubhouse (The Mainstay Inn). (HABS)

3. 635 Columbia Avenue, corner Stockton Place, (also called Little Howard Street on some maps). **Jackson's Clubhouse**, 1872, **(The Mainstay Inn)**: One of architect S.D. Button's finest surviving designs in Cape May. Built as an elegant gambling house for Southern gentlemen, its Italianate facade, pilastered cupola and gracefully columned veranda are certainly reminiscent of an antebellum structure. This American Bracketed Villa has one of Cape May's finest interiors, with 14 foot ceilings, original fixtures, and elaborate walnut furnishings. Bed & Breakfast Inn. Tour and Tea. Seasonal.

> *The Mainstay Inn property also includes the grey and beige house immediately next door. Notice the lovely landscaped flower garden areas, the rear yard lattice work, brick walkways, and the picket fence adjoining the two buildings. Directly across the street, The Officers' Quarters offers a successful mix of new to the original Mainstay properties.*

4. 631 Columbia, *Moses Simon Cottage*, ca. 1870 **(The Cottage)**: Intricately detailed, two level porch. Note deep roof cornice, interrupted in the center by a huge fan-shaped pediment–holdover of the French Second Empire style. Bed & Breakfast "extension" of the Mainstay.

Looking south down Columbia Street at this point, you may notice that building facades and open porches are all in line. Peek down through one porch for a view straight through all the porches toward the end of the block. Vacationing Victorians, eager to "see and be seen," loved this feature! Note differences and similarities in the roof lines, porch balustrades, brackets and carpenters' trim. At this point, you may wish to cross the street, to the corner of Guerney and Columbia for a good vantage point to view the variety of structures at this intersection.

5. 621 Columbia. E*van Morris House,* 1867-68 **(The Delsea):** Designed by S. D. Button. First quality example of restored ornamental bric-a-brac. Note the seawave-shaped trim of the second story porch rooftop. Porch columns and spandrel ornaments are of painted cast iron. Seasonal.

Cape Island Baptist Church.   *H. Michaels*

6. Cape Island Baptist Church, 1916, corner Columbia Avenue and Guerney Street: Spanish Revival style with stucco and red tile gable roof. The earlier Bible School structure was first built on property that was once part of the lawn of the Stockton Hotel. Main church and campanile were added in 1937.

John B. McCreary House (The Abbey). (HABS)

Stockton Place Row Houses.   *H. Michaels*

7. Corner Columbia and Guerney. *John B. McCreary House,* 1869-70 **(The Abbey)**: Designed by S.D. Button as an elegant summer villa for a wealthy Philadelphia coal baron. A stunning Gothic Revival house featuring a 60 foot tower, arched ruby-glass windows and elaborate carpenters' lace trim. (Note that no two sides of the house have the same style trim!) Original photos show vertical board and batten siding, small open side porches and a gazebo on the lawn. Owners, dedicated to the details of restoring the house to its original appearance, have restored the wrought iron cresting to the top of the tower and completely surrounded the property with the picket fencing of its original design. Bed & Breakfast Inn. Tour. Seasonal.

Make a left on Guerney Street and walk toward the beach.

8. Numbers 30, 28, 26, 24, 22, 20, 18 and 16 Guerney Street, 1869, **Stockton Place Row Houses or The Stockton Cottages,** (guesthouses and private residences): In 1869, $50,000 built this row of identical rental cottages located opposite and named in honor of the great Stockton Hotel. These charming Gothic Revival structures are typical examples of the "Cape May Cottage", distinguished by a wealth of wood ornamentation. Note the enormous acroterion at roof peaks, the carved vergeboards and spandrel arches filled with carpenters' lace. Several cottages have undergone major restorations and carry on the tradition of providing a retreat for vacationers: #30 (John Wesley Inn), #28 (The Gingerbread House) and #26 (The Belvidere). At printing, The Belvidere is a lone example of a time when most of Cape May's colorful Victorian structures were repainted white with green shutters!

Walk to corner and make a right onto Beach Drive.

9. Ocean Promenade (one block): Here is a lovely spot to stop and rest. Select one of the benches on the promenade along the edge of the beach and take in the view!

Make another right onto Ocean Street.

The Colonial Hotel.   *H. Michaels*

Evan Morris Cottage (The Seaview House).   *H. Michaels*

10. Corner Beach Drive and Ocean Street, *The Colonial Hotel,* 1894-95, **(The Inn of Cape May)**: Delightful survivor of Cape May's wooden hotel era. Originally built in the Second Empire mansard style, this structure has evolved into an eclectic building with Queen Anne witch-hat turrets and an Italianate style fifth floor added at a later date. Note lively textured surfaces in the vast expanses of fish scale shingles and clapboarding. Interior is of rooming house style with central hall and rooms to either side. Peek inside the lobby to view some of its original details such as a curved registration desk, two wooden spindle screens, staircase, fireplace and to the rear, a vintage hotel elevator. The lobby and expanses of the old dining areas have been transformed into an open-to-the-public antique shop. This structure is best viewed from across the street. Operating hotel, restaurant, bar/lounge and antique shop. Tour and tea. Seasonal.

Design #346
"Shoppwell's Modern
Houses", Vol. 1,

11. 19 Ocean Street, *Evan Morris Cottage,* 1877-88 **(Seaview House)**: Particularly interesting example of Second Empire mansard style, most likely built from a design which appeared in "Shopwell's Modern Houses", July 1886. This was a catalog of house patterns from which the discerning home builder of the 1880's could combine an infinite variety of mass-produced architectural details to "outdo" the neighbors.

Note details on:

> 22 Ocean Street (southside) **(Leith Hall Inn)**: Ruby and white stained glass medallion motif on front windows and doorway.
>
> 25 Ocean: **(Kelly's Celtic Inn)**: Ruby etched glass windows over front door.
>
> 23 Ocean (northside): *Beaver Cottage* **(Beauclaire's B & B)**: private residence: Beautifully restored structure with the teeniest of balconies stepping out from under a black witch-hat turret. The home is a showcase of typical Queen Anne elements: heavily textured facade - patterned shingles, carved gable ornamentation, spindles and stained glass panels around windows!

The four corners at Ocean Street and Columbia Avenue offer a wonderful spot to view Cape May as it remains intact since the early 1900's. Each direction affords an array of Victorian architectural examples and some striking restorations. Starting at the far corner, diagonally across the street:

The Douglas Gregory House (The Queen Victoria).   H. Michaels

12. 102 Ocean Street. The Douglas Gregory House, 1881 **(The Queen Victoria)**: Built by Delaware River pilot Douglas Gregory, on land which was the original site of the Columbia Hotel (which succumbed to the Great Fire of 1878). Through the years the house was leased to the Navy and also used as a Base Army Hospital. The small guesthouse in the rear was purchased and moved from a military base where the Cape May Coast Guard is now located. For many years, this Second Empire mansard home was used as a rooming house. Current owners undertook the impeccable restoration of the structure, spending nearly 6 months just to restore the exterior paint job alone! The cool greens and maroon accentuate the striking facade–note the corner window bays topped with a curved mansard roof, richly ornamented brackets and pillars of the front porch and the curved bannister leading down the front stairs. A true Victorian garden borders the house and its wrought iron fence. Bed and Breakfast Inn. Open all year. Christmas Tour. Special Events.

The Humphrey Hughes House.   H. Michaels

13. 101-103 Ocean Street, *Dr. Ware's Drugstore and Fountain* **(Cheek's Shop and The Queen's Hotel)**. One of the few remaining original Victorian storefronts in Cape May. Notice the deep blue/gray cornices supported by carved brackets, the steep mansard roofline with dormered windows and the jaunty striped awnings.

14. 29 Ocean Street, **The Humphrey Hughes House**, 1913: Today, a bed & breakfast inn named in honor of Captain Humphrey Hughes who sailed to Cape May in 1660 and was one of the original landowners of the town. This shingled Dutch Colonial Revival style house is distinguished by the unpainted shingles of its exterior and its grand uplifted veranda which sweeps three sides of the structure. The Columbia Avenue side of the house has four leaded stained glass windows. Bed & Breakfast Inn. Seasonal.

> Looking north up Columbia Avenue, notice the side and rear view of **The Abbey** with its rosette-patterned slate roof. No. 606 Columbia is also a part of The Abbey B & B property. Removal of its modern siding during restoration uncovered the intact clapboard.note the unusual tin mansard roof! Across the street at 609 Columbia Avenue is **The John Craig House**, a bed & breakfast inn with a wonderfully exotic Victorian style garden—visit this spot during the blooming season for a treat!

> *Return to the corner and look up at the variety of mansard rooftops, especially the wonderful mansard tower of the **Columbia House** (26 Ocean). Note the subtle Victorian color treatment of this charming seaside cottage.*

> *Continue on Ocean Street, going away from the beach.*

15. 107 Ocean Street, *The J. M. Gemrig House*, ca. 1888, **(The Queen's Cottage)**: An authentic Victorian garden fills the side yard of this charming Queen Anne style dwelling that is part of the Queen Victoria properties. The house exhibits an array of carpenters' lace, rosette ornamentation near the roofline, fish scale shingles and a great oversailing front porch. Note the lattice screen with arched doorway at the rear of the house, the tall decorated chimney and a striking variety of colors accenting the rich architectural details of the house.

16. 111 Ocean Street, *Captain Walden House*, 1892 **(The Fairthorne B & B)**: Built for a wealthy whaling captain. A Shingle style structure that almost looks seaworthy! Note the wide gambrel roof and the deck-like wrap-around porch "high and dry" above the street level. Bed & Breakfast Inn. Open all year.

17. 115 Ocean Street, 1880 (private residence). Built by local Cape May architect Enos Williams, this home is yet another one that survived a move from its original site on Lafayette Street. The original entrance is located on the Hughes Street side, in the earlier built rear section of the home. This stately, Gothic style house features a colorful array of wooden carpenter's trim, cut and applied to each side of the house in a fancy assortment of circles, triangles, sun-bursts, moonshapes, fan shapes and scrolls. The roof is detailed with twelve sets of brackets and the bay window (Hughes St.) offers a close view of the appliqued wooden trim topped with a rolled tin roof. Note lovely restored brick sidewalks, wrought iron fencing, Victorian gardens and gazebo. Private home.

Intersection of Ocean Street and Hughes Street

Dr. Phillips House (Captain Mey's Inn)

M. Cudworth

18. 202 Ocean Street, *Dr. Phillips House,* 1890 **(Captain Mey's Inn)**: One of the large doctor-owned structures which lined Ocean Street in the 1890's, when it was affectionately known as "doctors' row." Note the massive proportions, porch high above the street, the simple classic lines with the absence of lacy ornamentation. The interior boasts three Tiffany quality stained glass windows. Bed and Breakfast Inn. Christmas Tour. Open all year.

603-605 Hughes (Commercial Shop).

M. Cudworth

19. 603-605 Hughes, McCray's Pharmacy **(The Gingerbread Angel)**: A particularly important American Gothic storefront structure which still retains its original function. Note severely pointed roofline with large hanging pendant and carved bargeboards.

> *Make a right onto Hughes Street. Once classified as a "cow path", Hughes Street is now one of the most admired sections of Cape May. Today we find these two residential blocks virtually intact and unmarked by the 20th century. The street scene offers every distinguishable aspect of the small-town residential Victorian streetscape: gas-fired street lamps, slate and brick sidewalks, century-old trees, tiny gardens, picket and wrought-iron fences and gates, horse mounting blocks and hitching posts.*

Hitching posts, Hughes from 20 to 34.   *M. Cudworth*

20. 609 Hughes, *The Albert Henry Hughes House*, 1838 **(The Wooden Rabbit)**: The original and oldest section of this house was built to the rear of the property. This may very well be the oldest structure included in this tour. It is also reported that Robert E. Lee summered here! Country Bed & Breakfast Inn. Open all year.

21. 612 Hughes, **The Manor House**, ca. 1900: Built at the turn of the century as a wedding present for the daughter of a prominent N.Y. couple. Handsome example of the Shingled Dutch Colonial Revival style architecture. Note uniform use of unpainted wood shingles and the general elimination of fancy ornamentation. Bed & Breakfast Inn. Open all year.

22. 619 Hughes, **White Dove Cottage**: The mansard roof of this cottage with its hexagonal tiles and rosette design is impressive. Note the symmetry of design, curved and hooded dormers, elaborate chimneys and carpenters' trim. Bed & Breakfast inn. Open all year.

23. 629 Hughes, **Cape May Cottage**: This house sports three hanging rooftop pendants, sawtooth and fish scale shingles and some lovely porch detailing with fan-shaped brackets topping each column.

212 Stockton Place (The Bell Bungalow).   M. Cudworth

24. 633 Hughes, A very masculine-looking house with strong angular lines. Notice the tiny "pulpit-like" balcony almost at ground level!

> *At the corner of Hughes Street and Stockton Place, make a short detour onto Stockton Place.*

25 and 26. 215 Stockton Place, (N.E. corner Hughes Street) and 212 Stockton Place, **The Bell Bungalow** (at the rear of The Mainstay): These are two delightful examples of the Bungalow Style building which originated in British India as way stations for travelers. Popular in this country between 1900-1920, these buildings were economical to build and were especially prevalent in California and at seaside resorts. No. 215 has gothic arch molding in windows and built-in porch seats. Don't miss the gazebo on the side lawn! No. 212 has unusual tapered porch posts. Look above this cottage for a view of The Mainstay's cupola. Private residences.

Return to Hughes Street.

27. 637 Hughes, *The Cherry House*, 1849 (private residence): The property was part of a large tract owned by Lemuel Leaming, an early landowner in Cape May, whose family was noted for its development of Cape May County. The original front porch has been removed and the front entranceway has typical elements of the Federal style: note paneled door topped by semicircular fanlight. The original front door is on the sun porch.

The Joseph Hall House. (HABS)

28. 645 Hughes, *The Joseph Hall House*, 1868 (private residence): One of the most striking and imaginative color combinations in town (mustard yellow and blue)–witness the exceptional carpenters' embellishment: intricate tendrils of the vergeboard (not found in any other building in Cape May), the carved acroteria, hooded dormers and open lattice pillars of the front porch. Fan brackets and the family name are hand-carved into the front screen door. Notice the lovely motif of the wrought iron fencing and the original birdhouse perched in the side garden. See cover photograph!

29. 644 Hughes, *The Baltimore Hotel*, ca. 1867 **(The Girls' Friendly Society)**: This building is the last of the surviving intown old wooden hotels. Its size, height and general plainness typifies many other early hostelries of the era. (Later hotels were erected nearer to the beach.) In 1896, the building was acquired by the Episcopal Church and still operates as a well-kept summer holiday residence for young women. Seasonal.

30. 651 Hughes, **The Damback House**, ca. 1865 (private residence): Charming cottage with a delightful example of how the early 1900's addition of "indoor plumbing" was done—note the tiny room on stilts added to the side of the house, complete with fanciful bric-a-brac trim and bright squares of stained glass in the windows! Tiny grape arbor on the left still offers a cool retreat from the summer sun.

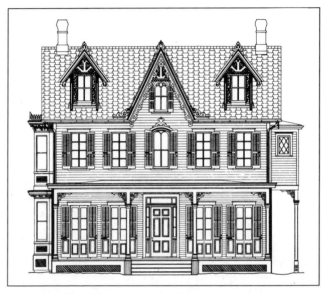

(Stratton Ware House (HABS)

31. 655 Hughes, *J. Stratton Ware House*, (private residence): Handsome Gothic cottage of the 1860's displaying the high artistic level of Cape May's carpenter-builders. Lots of skillful woodworking here in the many layers of ornamentation—look up at the wonderfully elaborate vergeboards, acroterion, cornices and incised hooded moldings above the topmost windows.

32. 657-659 Hughes, *J. K. Stites Cottage*, 1869-70 (private residence): Notable double cottage with many early additions to its simple original parallelogram shape: deep bays on second floor, third story gable, cornices and a large first floor porch.

33. 665 Hughes, **The Franklin House**, (private residence): Modest and sweet—a lovely home with elements that add to the charm of the Victorian streetscape—nicely detailed front porch, complete with rambling wisteria, rocking chairs, fan-shaped carvings on front door, third story gothic window, picket fencing, and at the curb, a horse mount and hitching post!

34. 664 Hughes, (private residence): Impressive restoration of a lovely Gothic Revival home–note the fanciful paint job of rose pinks and white with blue shutters. Unusual circular motif in porch balustrades. Typical picket fencing and severe gothic pointed roofline with pointed dormer windows.

At intersection of Hughes and Franklin Streets: The row cottages here on Franklin Street, facing Hughes (Nos. 515-50-9) are on property that was once part of the Corgie Plantations prior to 1853. These simple homes are typical early structures–long and narrow, yet displaying notable details. No. 515 has a delightful wrought iron fence with a whimsical daisy design. No 511 (The **William and Margaret Cottage**, B & B guesthouse) was built in 1869 with "three rooms down and three rooms up and a fine wrap-around porch". Note the lovely gardens tucked around the property and the birdhouses on facade of house.

803 Columbia.

H. Michaels

Make a right onto Franklin Street and proceed one block towards the beach. Intersection of Franklin Street and Columbia Avenue.

35. 803 Columbia, (private residence): A large piece of property still borders this cottage on the left side corner of Franklin Street. Stylishly painted maroon, gray and tan, this Queen Anne structure is notable for its unusual detail visible from this side view: grid-like spindle bracketing, original iron cresting over side bay windows, small squares of stained glass in upper window sashes.

Look across Columbia Avenue to view:

J. F. Jacoby House (The Dormer House International).

36. 800 Columbia, *J. F. Jacoby House,* 1899 **(The Dormer House International)**: Delightful gardens originally surrounded this two-corner property with its stately, large columned house. Note the simpler, more severe line of the Colonial Revival style, popular after the 1876 Centennial Exposition. Guesthouse. Open all year.

> *Make a right turn onto Columbia Avenue for a view of more of its delightful cottages.*

37. 733 Columbia, **(Twin Gable B & B Inn)** and private residence: Example of the Cape May double cottage; one of the Peter McCollum development houses.

> Note: 722 Columbia **(Henry Sawyer B & B Inn)**, 1875: Former residence of Henry Sawyer while he built the Chalfonte Hotel (see site #1).

38. 712 Columbia, *J. Spicer Leaming House,* ca. 1879 **(The Belmont)**: The land on which this house stands was originally owned in 1876 by Henry Sawyer (original owner of the Chalfonte Hotel to the rear of this house). A handsome cottage with embellished, hooded dormers and a permanent porch awning. Guesthouse. Seasonal.

39. 729 Columbia, 1871 **(Tismyin)**: A stately, symmetrical structure with Italianate influence–note flattened roofline, cornice overhang and brackets. Property fronted with wrought iron fencing.

40. 725 Columbia, *John Benizot House*, 1872 **(Linda Lee B&B Inn)**: Cape May's noteworthy architect Stephen Decatur Button designed a number of similar cottages on Columbia Avenue that were erected and sold by McCollum, a local entrepreneur. This structure, together with neighbors, 719 (Brass Bed) and 715 (Victorian Rose), share that distinction. Note the pointed Gothic windows and a nice evening view of ruby etched glass around front door. Open all year.

Lewis Tannenbaum House (The Brass Bed).   *Evelyn Zuckerman*

41. 719 Columbia, *Lewis Tannenbaum House*, ca. 1872 **(The Brass Bed)**: Of Gothic Revival style, this house has many distinctive features, such as the third-story central gable with large hanging pendant, dormered windows, carved vergeboards and paired cornice brackets. This cottage has been impressively restored using warm Victorian exterior colors with a very innovative treatment of painted ornamentation to accent the architectural details! Bed and Breakfast Inn. Christmas Tour. Open all year.

Washington St.
Jefferson St.
Page St.
Pearl St.
Cogue St.
Sewell Ave.
McCullum St.
Benton Ave.
Kearny Ave.
Stockton Ave.
Queen St.

Jefferson St.
Beach Ave.

COLUMBIA AVE
HUGHES ST

Howard St.
Kearny Ave.
Stockton Pl.
Gurney St.

Franklin St.
Lafayette St.
Elmira St.

Ocean St.

Bank St.

66 67

Decatur St.
63 64 65   68 69   70
62 59 56 55 54

Chestnut

Jackson St.
61 60 58 57   53
Start   52
42   52

Perry St.
44 43

Claghorn Pl.
North St.
St. Lafayette St.
Congress Pl.
Washington St. Mall
Carpenters Lane

45
46

Congress St.
49   50 51
48 47

Windsor St.

Grant St.
Beach Ave.

**Site Guide
Walking Tour
Loop B**

N
E
W
S

WALKING TOUR
LOOP B: SITES 42-70

The Eldridge Johnson House (The Pink House). (HABS)

42. 33 Perry Street, corner Carpenters' Lane, *The Eldridge Johnson House*, ca.1882 **(The Pink House)**: One of Cape May's most photographed houses, a three tiered "wedding cake delight", with layers of that gingerbread trim for which Cape May is nationally known. Built after the fire of 1878 which destroyed this section of Cape May, this Gothic Revival house (originally at 225 Congress–site of today's Victorian Motel) was moved here in the late 1960's. Also note the beautiful ruby glass above the front door. Gift shop and private residence. Seasonal.

Congress Hall.   *M. Cudworth*   *H. Michaels*

Dr. Henry Hunt House.   *M. Cudworth*

43. Congress Hall, bordered by Perry Street, Congress Place, Congress Street and Beach Drive, 1879, with latter additions: The present Congress Hall is the third building on this site to have the same name. The first was built in 1816 by Thomas Hughes, the first man of Cape May County to be elected to Congress. The form of Congress Hall is typical of many late 19th century resort hotels: L-shaped with a multi-story colonnade that is a hallmark of Cape May hotels. This structure was rebuilt in brick (the first two wooden hotels succumbed to fires) and was host to a string of political figures such as Presidents Harrison, Grant, and Pierce in the days when Cape May was known as "the Playground for Presidents". President Harrison set up Congress Hall as his summer White House. A later addition to the building designed by S. D. Button, included the 100 foot wing parallel to the ocean with a music pavilion on the lawn where J. Philip Sousa gave concerts and was inspired to write "The Congress Hall March"!

> NOTE: At time of printing, Congress Hall is in the process of a major renovation. Public ground floor areas have been transformed into gift shops, the ballroom into a café, and "sneak preview" tours are available.

44. 209 Congress Place, *Dr. Henry Hunt House*, 1881 (private residence): Erected on property that was once part of the Congress Hall rear lawns. Affectionately nicknamed "Grandfather's Eclectic" by its present owner, this home displays features from Queen Anne, Mansard, Stick, Italianate and Gothic Revival styles! Note the mixed building materials, patterns, textures and colors on the same facade. Notable features include the fanciful belvedere with turned-wood columns (the largest in town), the scissor truss on the gable and the stained glass first floor windows.

The Joseph Evans House (HABS).

The E.C. Knight House. (HABS).

45 and 46. 207 Congress Place, *The Joseph Evans House,* 1881-82 and its neighbor, 203 Congress Place, The *E. C. Knight House,* 1882-83 (private residences): Two handsome examples of domestic suburban architecture–the American Bracketed Villa, S. D. Button is credited with building the Evans and most probably the extremely similar Knight cottage. Of typical Button design, the houses are open and inviting with large walk-through windows, double front doors, prominent two-story verandas at front and rear. Italianate decorative elements–large overhanging eaves with brackets, iron cresting on roof.

> *Follow the brick sidewalk on Congress Place, making a right turn around the corner to Congress Street (side view of E. C. Knight House) and walk one block to South Lafayette Street. Stop and view:*

47 and 48. 111-113 Congress Place, (corner S. Lafayette), *Joseph Leedom Houses,* 1887 (private residences): These cottages display many delightful medieval elements which are the hallmarks of the Queen Anne style. For instance, note the extensive use of fish-scale shingle, complex masses of structure, tiny porches tucked in at all levels and massive towers topped with witch-hat turrets. For a dramatic show of light and shadow, view the houses early to mid-morning on a sunny day.

Joseph Leedom Houses.   M. Cudworth

The Neafie-Levy House. (HABS)

View across the street.

49. 38-30 Congress Street, corner Congress Place, *The Neafie-Levy House*, 1865-66 (private residence): Owner Jacob Neafie sold half of this double house to John Levy, business partner and fellow Philadelphian in 1867. The very early structure is a textbook example of the Cape May cottage built in the years just following the Civil War–symmetrical, emphasized cupola and a two-story veranda that hides most of the facade. The tangled web of vines, hedges and trees surrounding the house give it a very mysterious air! Notice the delightful fringed oriental-style cupola on the rooftop and the lacy wrought iron fencing surrounding the property. Twin stable structure at rear of property.

Turn around and go back, retracing steps on Congress Street heading toward beach.

50 and 51. 22 and 24 Congress Street, *The Joseph and John Steiner Cottages*, ca. 1848-51, (private residences): These cottages are among Cape May's earliest summer homes and their presence may mark the appearance of the "summer resort cottage" popularly common in Ocean Grove, New Jersey, and also later at Sea Grove (Cape May Point). It was reported that the two cottages were built by a Southern summer visitor, presumably for each of his two daughters. Originally, the second-story front porches were connected. Notice the large hanging pendants, stylized acroteria, the variety of carpenters' lace and fancy porch balustrades.

> *Continue on Congress Street to Beach Drive and make a left. Walk across the front of Congress Hall toward Perry Street. View Congress Hall front and lawn areas. Look across the lawn for a nice view of the yellow and white Evans house and gray and white Knight house. Walk along Beach Drive in front of Congress Hall and make a left on Perry Street for a quick detour to view:.*

52. 9 Perry Street, *Fryers' Cottage*, 1879 **(King's Cottage)**: An unusual ceramic porch railing makes this Second Empire house with Stick-style ornamentation even more distinctive. Originally designed by Frank Furness (Physick Estate) and George Hewitt in 1871, it was rebuilt to the same specifications after the fire of 1878. The unique glazed tiles of flower and coin design are believed to have come from a pavilion of the Centennial Exposition of 1876 in Philadelphia. Guesthouse. Seasonal.

Fryer's Cottage **(King's Cottage)**. *(Habs)*

Note: 29 Perry Street, **(Perry Street Inn)** is on the original site of the *Ocean House* (1840) where the Great Fire of 1878 began.

Retrace steps back to Beach Drive make a left. Go one block to Jackson Street and make another left. On your way, view the "Seven Sister" cottages on Atlantic Terrace, looking above and behind the "Akroteria" food stands. Jackson Street has a remarkable array of architectural styles and there is a lot of dynamic energy on this street today!

The Seven Sisters. 20 Jackson (Holly House).   M. Cudworth

53. 10, 12, 16, 18 and 20 Jackson Street, **(The Seven Sisters)**, 1891-92: Seven identical structures designed by S. D. Button on the site of The Atlantic Hotel which succumbed to the fire of 1878. (Two of the seven cottages are behind Jackson Street on Atlantic Terrace and may be viewed between Nos. 12 and 16.) The buildings are of the Renaissance Revival style which imitated urban Italian palaces of the 16th and 17th centuries. The demand for privacy and quiet resulted in the innovative idea of fronting the buildings on a courtyard (Atlantic Terrace) and making the principal street (Jackson) a rear entrance. Solid and dignified, The Seven Sisters exhibit lovely details, moldings with rosettes and unusual hooded roof over front bay windows. Note wrought iron fencing and rear (Jackson Street) gardens. Each interior houses a beautiful three-story spiral staircase. Guesthouses and private residences.

John C. McConnell House. (HABS)

54. 15 Jackson Street, *John C. McConnel House*, 1883: Constructed on the site of the Knickerbocker Hotel after the 1878 fire. Exhibits the variety of surface textures, half-timber overlays and pronounced asymmetry which are hallmarks of the Queen Anne style. Summer rental.

The George Hildreth House (Poor Richard's Inn).   H. Michaels

55. 17 Jackson Street, *The George Hildreth House*, 1882 **(Poor Richard's Inn)**: Built as a private residence for the original owner of the neighboring Carroll Villa Hotel (important structure as it served as a model for the later Gallagher House at 45 Jackson). The house is of the French-inspired Second Empire style–note the symmetry at each level, the three dimensional effect with projecting and receding surfaces and the classic ornamentation. A popular guesthouse today, this restored structure had 1600 pieces of multi-colored roof slate replaced by the owners! Seasonal.

The Carroll Villa Hotel.   circa 1910

56. 19 Jackson Street, *The Carroll Villa Hotel,* 1882, **(The Mad Batter Restaurant and Carroll Villa Hotel)**: Originally a rooming house which catered to Baltimore clientele and was named in honor of Maryland's longest-surviving signer of the Declaration of Independence. Similar in detail to the Chalfonte Hotel, it is also an American Bracketed Villa. The north wing was added to the side of the building in 1895. Notice flattened roof topped by a very fancy cupola, complete with brackets, arched moldings and finials. Restaurant and Hotel. Seasonal.

57. 22 Jackson Street, *Harry Parker Cottage,* ca. 1900, **(Inn at 22 Jackson)**: Marvelous detail in the turned spindles, tri-clustered corner porch columns, carved brackets and porch balustrade. Note octagonal tower set asymmetrically ala Queen Anne style and outstanding multi-color paint job. Victorian suites and cottages.

58. 24 Jackson Street, *The George Baum House,* 1905 **(The Windward House)**: Large, unique, American Shingle Style building exhibiting an intriguing array of window treatments. Restorative process uncovered original shingles in good condition under asbestos siding which was commonly applied to "modernize" the Victorian houses years ago. Structural detailing combines Colonial and Queen Anne styles and includes massive porch supports, projecting bays and dormer windows. Interior includes fine collection of stained and beveled glass. Edwardian style Bed and Breakfast Inn. Open all year.

59. 22 Jackson Street, *Ebbit House*, 1879 **(The Virginia)**: One of the first hotels to be built on Jackson Street after the 1878 fire. Expansive example of the American Bracketed Villa with some Italianate decorative elements: low pitched roof with overhanging eaves and large brackets for supports, prominent verandas, large walk-through first floor windows and a wealth of carpenters' lace. Guestrooms, restaurant and small bar. Open all year.

60. 38 Jackson Street, *I Leaming Sheppard House*, 1896 **(The Prince Edward)**: Handsome example of a classic Queen Anne style cottage with Colonial Revival detailing. The home features a large variety of original stained glass windows including what is believed to be the largest working stained glass window in Cape May (on first floor landing–lovely viewed at night!) Victorian suites with kitchens. Seasonal.

61. 42 Jackson Street, The J. Henry Edmonds House, ca. 1879 **(The Merry Widow)**: Exciting 20th century interpretation of the Victorian multi-color exterior paint job. Note the variety of surface treatments of the modified Queen Anne structure with a Mansard roof: the turned wood porch columns, asymmetrical masses with large castle turrets and note how the curved porch accentuates all the curves of the building. Observe porch steps with incised design. Apartments and commercial stores.

I. Leaming Sheppard House (The Prince Edward)　　　*Clinton A. Scott*

62. 45 Jackson Street, *Christopher Gallagher House*, 1882-83 (private residence): Identical to 17 Jackson **(Poor Richard's Inn)** with an extended porch and reception hall altered by local contractors in 1905. Multi color paint accentuates the carved woodwork of this Second Empire style home, and the tall mansard roof provides a full story at attic level. Notice lovely detail painting on the porch ceiling, multi-color slate roof and intricate lattice work on porch.

Make right turn onto Carpenter's Lane. Walk one block to Decatur Street and make a right heading toward beach.

63. 132 Decatur Street, corner Carpenter's Lane. *Aaron Roseman House*, ca. 1895 (private residence): As you walk alongside this house, notice the large stained glass window on the Carpenter's Lane side (best viewed at night). This house closely resembles the Harry Parker cottage (22 Jackson). Both facades are filled with intricately turned spindles and an octagonal tower.

64. 130 Decatur Street, *James Leaming House*, 1895 (apartments): The narrow lot indicates the increased density of the town at the turn of the century. The bold arch supported by brackets over the central window is quite unusual. The corner tower with its rounded windows accentuate the house's asymmetry.

65. 122 Decatur Street (private residence): This tiny cottage has special appeal–lovely soft colors of gray and mauve, lacy gingerbread, and a charming gothic window at its peak with shutters outstretched like open arms. A true doll house!

66. 501 Hughes Street, N.W. corner Decatur, *Thomas Williamson Cottage*, ca. 1885 **(Bell Shields Guesthouse)**: Another typical Cape May cottage with a fish-scale shingled upper story, stained glass panels in second floor windows and an elaborate porch derived from the Queen Anne style.

Take a peek down this end of Hughes Street. Note the long and narrow cottage with Z-shaped cut-outs at roof overhang. This carpenters' lace throws an interesting shadow configuration when viewed in the late afternoon.

Cape Island Presbyterian Church.   *H. Michaels*

67. N.E. corner of Hughes and Decatur, **Cape Island Presbyterian Church**, 1898: The congregation's third house of worship in Cape May—one former Presbyterian church is now the Cape May Welcome Center on Lafayette Street. A strongly symmetrical building with an interesting and lovely interior architecturally focused on the altar. Notice the large scale Gothic Revival characteristics: steep roofline, tower with hooded windows, leaded stained glass windows and massive bargeboards with a truss that repeats the gothic arch. The arch and the keyhole shapes are repeated as a motif throughout this handsome structure.

68. 114 Decatur, 1886 (private residence): Common summer resort structure—this cottage still retains the white and green paint job that was the typical reaction against the brighter Victorian color combinations of the late 1800's.

> *As you head toward the Beach promenade, look to either side of Decatur Street—to your left on Columbia Avenue is the lovely side view of the Queen Victoria Inn. To your right, through the parking lot of Watson's Merion Inn, is a good rear view of the Carroll Villa with its fancy cupola and its next door neighbor, Poor Richard's Inn.*

Watson's Merion Inn. *M. Cudworth*

69. 106 Decatur Street, **Watson's Merion Inn**, 1885 (restaurant): In 1885, Patrick Collins opened his marine boarding villa "convenient to the Iron Pier and big hotels". By 1900 it evolved to Collin's Cafe. Since 1900 this building and property have undergone many changes during almost a century of restaurant service. Original photos show an outdoor tree-shaded beer garden surrounded by a picket fence, a separate entrance for ladies and two-story front porches. Also out front is one of the few remaining mounting blocks and hitching posts.

70. Corner Decatur and Beach Drive, *Denizot's Ocean View House*, 1879 **(Restaurants, Spiaggi's and Katie O'Brien's Pub)**: This four-story building was originally a small hotel, bathhouse and restaurant. While the Ocean View House was being erected, Mr. Denizot was also building the Iron Pier, an iron amusement pier constructed directly across the street, stretching out several hundred feet over the ocean! Note the original bracketed cupola and the large two-story bay.

Cross over Beach Drive and find an empty bench on the Promenade–a perfect way to end this walking tour–taking in fresh ocean breezes and a wonderful view of the beach, the Atlantic Ocean and Cape May's beach front structures.

NOTE:
Now that you have taken the walking tours, discover historic Cape May on your own. The entire city of Cape May was declared a National Landmark in 1976 and holds the distinction of having the largest extant collection of 19th century frame buildings in the United States today! Because of space limitations, we were unable to include every noteworthy structure in this tour. So, with the aid of this guide and street map, take another time for a leisurely exploration by yourself. Corgie Street behind the Washington Avenue post office is particularly charming. This little neighborhood offers tiny lanes (no cars) weaving in and out between Franklin and Jefferson Streets with a wealth of Victorian cottages. On the opposite end of town, the neighborhood to the south-west of Perry Street–Congress, Windsor, Grant, North Street and South Lafayette have many more charming examples from the past. Enjoy!

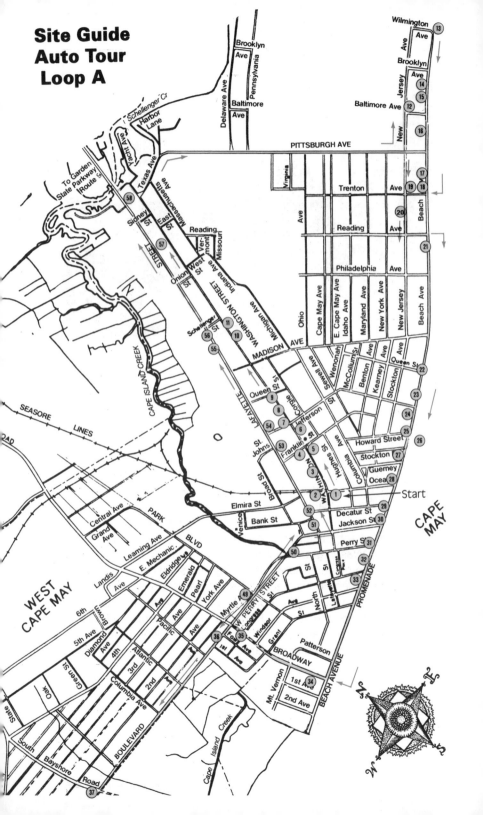

Site Guide
Auto Tour
Loop A

AUTO TOUR
LOOP A: SITES 1-37

This Auto Tour will give you a good overall view of the city layout, as well as an opportunity to view many outstanding and varied architectural examples which are spread throughout the town beyond the perimeters of the Main Historic District. We will begin in the very center of town and make a large loop, taking in the sights on the way to the northeast end of town (Poverty Beach area), then along Beach Drive to Broadway, which is the border of West Cape May. We will then head out of town down to Cape May Point for a view of this residential resort which was known as Sea Grove in the 1800's.

LOOP A: CAPE MAY CITY

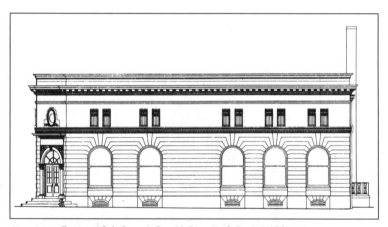

New Jersey Trust and Safe Deposit Co. (McDowell's Gallery) (HABS)

1. Begin tour at: Corner Ocean and Washington Streets. *New Jersey Trust and Safe Deposit Company*, 1895 **(McDowell's Gallery)**: This dignified Renaissance Revival building once served as Cape May's City Hall. Note large Roman arched windows and the heavily decorated belt courses dividing each differently finished story of this handsome structure. Art Gallery and gifts. Open all year.

M. Cudworth

Joseph Hughes House (Alexander's). Renovations include extended porches and dining areas.

St. John's Episcopal Church. (HABS)

2. Corner Ocean and Washington Street, *St. Mary's Roman Catholic Church*, 1911 **(Our Lady, Star of the Sea Church)**: A late example of the American Romanesque Revival Style displaying distinctive characteristics in the use of rounded arches for doors and windows. Impressive interior includes vast plastered walls and a breadth as wide as it is high.

> *Proceed on Washington Street, heading away from the Mall. This section includes a variety of restored Victorian structures, housing antique and specialty gift shops. Note earthy paint job on #660.*

3. 653 Washington Street, *Joseph Hughes House*, ca. 1880 **(Alexander's)**: Lovely Second Empire cottage with classic ornamentation and a deep mansard roof, providing a full story at attic level. Original porches have been extended to wrap around structure.Note original wrought iron fencing, the variety of roof top shingles and wrap-around porch. Restaurant and Bed & Breakfast Inn. Seasonal. Tour.

> *Take time to explore the tiny structure behind Alexander's which houses the Cape May Historical Society Museum. Considered to date ca. 1775, the house retains the original wide tongue and groove floorboards and some original window glass. This structure once stood in the front portion of the lot now occupied by Alexander's.*

4. Cape May Firemen's Museum, 1983: A wonderful example of the new blending in with the old. This relatively recent structure features an intriguing display of antique fire equipment, depicting the history of Cape May's Fire Department. Open daily.

> NOTE: The northwest corner of Washington and Franklin streets welcomes a fine example of a brand new structure which blends into the Victorian neighborhood around it!

5. S.E. corner Washington and Franklin Streets, *St. John's Episcopal Church*, 1867-68, **(Church of the Advent)**: Gothic style church designed in the shape of a Greek cross. Features original board and batten siding over field stone foundation. Original stained glass windows.

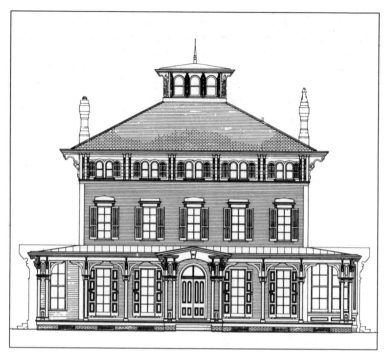

George Allen House. (HABS)

6. 720 Washington Street (next to Post Office), *George Allen House*, 1863-64 **(The Southern Mansion)**: A stunningly restored structure of national importance – its American Bracketed Villa design is credited to prominent American architect, Samuel Sloan, whose architectural pattern-book styles were popular in the 1800's. This particular house was styled after Sloan's "Southern Mansion" design. A remarkable example noted for its profuse ornamentation and generous scale, the structure features overhanging eaves supported by five foot high brackets, prominent verandas with elaborately bracketed columns and an enormous cupola. The interior boasts gas burning fireplaces decorated with marble and tile, fifteen foot ceilings sporting foot-deep cornices and moldings.

Author's Note: A recent tour of this property revealed many interesting facts about the property and restoration. The original owner, George Allen (Philadelphia lawyer, entrepreneur, department store owner), was instrumental in bringing the railroad system to Cape May and actually routed the tracks to run directly in front of his property. Many of the original furnishings (still present) were easily delivered directly to the house by train from Philadelphia!

7. 801 Washington Street, corner Jefferson, ca. 1840 **(The Washington Inn)**: Victorians thought nothing of moving their houses about. For example, this early plantation house was moved back to the rear corner of this property and later back to its present site! Early photos show the original facade with columns reaching to the third floor. Note giant 100 year old Japanese cryptomearia trees out front. Restaurant. Seasonal.

The Duke of Windsor.   M. Cudworth

8. 815 Washington Street, *James Hildreth House,* 1885 **(John Sudak Funeral Home)**: Austere, late Queen Anne house of Cape May's onetime mayor, James E. Hildreth. Note interesting repetition of angles in the pointed gables, slate roof, window hood and central tower.

9. 817 Washington Street, ca. 1896 **(The Duke of Windsor)**: Classic late Victorian home on a grand scale. Interior features three story carved oak staircase, corner fireplaces, ornate plaster ceilings and heavy paneled walls. Bed & Breakfast Inn. Seasonal.

NOTE: 821 Washington, ca. 1845 **(The Sheerer's)**. Wonderful showcase of a "carpenter's Gothic" cottage style. Private residence.

The Emlen Physick Estate. (HABS)

10. 1048 Washington Street, 1878-79 **(The Emlen Physick House and Estate)**: Impressive Stick Style house designed by the renowned architect, Frank Furness. Of highly individualistic design, this structure displays Furness' interest in richly colored patterns, highlights and shadows, steeply gabled roofs, hooded dormers and massive upside-down chimneys. Note deep textural siding decorated with the exposed beams and braces typical of the Stick Style. Deserted for many years, the building and property has been refurbished and fully restored to its former splendor. The present estate includes four of the original twenty-two acres and nine outbuildings. The 18 room house is open to the public as a museum and contains an extensive collection of original Victorian furnishings, clothing, books, toys, tools and artifacts. Tour. Open all year.

11. 1050 Washington Street, 1876 **(Carriage House)**: Built on the Physick Estate property two years before construction of the main house. Today it is home to the Cape May County Art League.

> *Continue on Washington Street, bearing right at the small triangle. Follow signs for BEACH. Pass Texas Avenue and follow the road as it curves to the right. One block before Beach Drive, make a left onto New Jersey Avenue. At the time of printing, this entire block was bare having been the site of the newly demolished Christian Admiral Hotel..*

12. 1500 New Jersey Avenue (Blue and white house with front facing Baltimore Avenue) *Dr. R. Walter Starr cottage*, 1906 (private residence): Important as the first house to be built in the new East Cape May tract. Note symmetry of structure, porch column detailing and high pitched gabled roof.

> *Stay on New Jersey Avenue to the end and make a right on Wilmington. This section is newly developed East Cape May area. Stop at beach for a lovely view.*

13. "Poverty Beach" : This beach area on left was known to be used by the hired help in Cape May's early days.

NOTE: The land northeast of Wilmington Avenue to the harbor was the object of a grand plan in the early 1900's to develop a new city east of Cape May: five thousand acres of land from the marshes, 7,500 building lots to be sold, grand hotels to be built and a major industrial seaport to be created. Major problems of every kind, including bankruptcy of the Cape May Real Estate Company and other individual early 19th century capitalists, halted the full East Cape May development. The homes west of this area to Madison Avenue were part of this original plan. Today, the major portion of this land is still undeveloped.

> *Turn right onto Beach Drive and continue along toward the center of Cape May. Many houses facing the ocean in this area were built on a grand scale and exemplify an architectural variety of period revivals such as Georgian, Spanish and Tudor styles. A number of interesting "hybrids" can also be noted as well as many shingled Dutch Colonial Revival homes.*

14. 1507 Beach Drive, *William J. Sewell, Jr. House*, 1912 (private residence): A lovely Shingle Style house reflecting great sensitivity to the seashore lifestyle of Cape May. Its L-shape provides maximum light and ventilation.

George W. Boyd House. (HABS)

15. 1501 Beach Drive, *George W. Boyd House,* 1911 (private residence): A grand scale Georgian Revival home displaying prominent symmetrical design, fanlight and sidelights around main door and entry portico.

16. Corner Beach Drive and Pittsburgh Avenue, former site of the *Hotel Cape May,* 1905-08 **(The Christian Admiral Hotel)**: This recently demolished hotel stood six-stories high and was of French Baroque style with influences of the more urban Atlantic City hotels. This grand hotel originally opened with 350 rooms, a fabulous lobby wainscotted in sienna marble and a roof garden.

17. 1307 Beach Drive, *Star Villa* 1884-85 **(Morning Star Villas)**: Originally a small three-story cottage type hotel that once stood at 10 Ocean Street (across from The Inn at Cape May - now a parking lot). Slated for demolition, it was bought by Dr. McIntire and moved to its present location in the 1960's. A fourth floor was added. The site has been recently restored and renovated as a condominium complex. Noteworthy are the variety of carpenters trim, fancy shingles and the repeated star motif.

18. 1301-1303 Beach Drive, *Peter Shields House,* 1906-07 **(Peter Shields Inn)**. A Georgian Revival mansion designed as a summer home for Peter Shields, one of the owners of the East Cape May Real Estate Company. This grand example reflected the expected splendor of the development in the East Cape May area, as many thought Cape May would eventually rival Newport, Rhode Island. This structure once housed the Cape May Tuna Club.

Turn right on Trenton Avenue.

William Weightman House. (HABS)

19. 5 Trenton Avenue, *William Weightman House*, 1850 **(Angel of the Sea)**: This impressive mansion was designed for Weightman, a Philadelphia chemist who invented quinine! Originally built at Washington and Franklin Streets (site of present post office), this Second Empire mansard structure was moved in 1881 to an ocean view at the corner of Ocean Street and Beach Drive. It remained here for nearly a century, sporting a new tower and corner entrance. In 1963 the house was moved here to its third site. Extensive and exacting restoration of the property took place in 1988 with recent owners. Bed & Breakfast Inn. Open all year.

Turn left on New Jersey Avenue. Cross over Reading Avenue to view on right.

Nelson Z. Graves House. (The Mission Inn).   *Edith Hewitt*

20. 1117 New Jersey Avenue, *Nelson Z. Graves House*, 1910-12 **(The Mission Inn)**. Designed by Philadelphia architect Lloyd W. Titus as a summer home for Graves (co-owner of the East Cape May Realty Company). In the 1940's, the home flourished with a dramatic flair under the ownership of Dr. Bob Redpath, in its unique setting opposite the Cape May Summer Theater. As a patron of the arts, "Dr. Bob" hosted many dinner parties at his home, attended by Broadway and Hollywood stars. Guests of the house have included Sarah Bernhart, Diana Barrymore, Tyrone Power, Gloria Swanson and Errol Flynn! Present owners have restored the building to its original charm in the California Mission/Spanish Colonial tradition, retaining the many outstanding features of this style: wrap-around terra-cotta tiles, columned and latticed pergola, stained glass windows and Flemish-style gable. Bed and Breakfast Inn. Open all year; winter weekends.

> *Turn left on Madison Avenue. Go one block and make a right on Beach Drive.*

21. 1005 Beach Drive, *Kate McCreary House*, 1923-34 (private residence). Its massive three dimensional nature inspired its local nickname–The Mae West House!

22. Note large Shingle Style homes in the Queen Street area. Note numbers 933 and 931.

The Sea Mist (and beach front houses).   H. Michaels

23. 927 Beach Drive, **(The Sea Mist)**: A fanciful tiered structure which actually looks seaworthy–could we call this "Steamboat Style" architecture?

24. 805 Beach Drive, *Henry Tatham House*, 1872-73 **(Stockton Villa)**: Another handsome mansarded cottage designed by Stephen D. Button.

25. Corner Beach Drive and Howard Street, **(The Hotel Macomber)**, ca. 1918: A four-story classic example of the Shingle Style building, popular in the late 19th and early 20th century at beach resorts on the East and West coasts. A structure of massive proportions, it was built on less than one-fifth of the original site of the famous Stockton Hotel (demolished in 1911). Hotel, restaurant and commercial shops. Seasonal.

26. Convention Hall.

27. Beach Theater.

28. Corner Beach Drive and Ocean Street, *The Colonial Hotel*, 1894-95 **(The Inn at Cape May)**: An interesting fact –Wallis Warfield (who later became the Dutchess of Windsor) had her "coming out" party here in 1917. This intersection offers a lovely view of Ocean Street, almost as if time has stood still since the 1800's. The southwest corner was the site of the Weightman House (site 19) and the Star Villa Hotel (site 17).

29. Corner Beach Drive and Decatur Street. *Denizot's Ocean View House* **(Restaurants Spiaggi's and Katie O'Brien's Pub)** 1879: Directly opposite, stretching out into the Atlantic, was the site of the old iron amusement pier. (now Arcade).

30. Jackson Street. One of Cape May's earliest streets. The original site of the Atlantic Hotel (ca. 1800). Look down street to view Seven Sister cottages (1891-92) and the Carroll Villa Hotel (1882).

Seven Sisters Cottages.

Look behind the Akroteria food stands for the above view taken from a 1907 scene of Cape May.

31. Perry Street. One of the first two public roads to be laid out on Cape Island.

32. Congress Hall. One of the few remaining 19th century resort hotels, which played host to many U.S. presidents– President Harrison setting up his summer White House here in 1890-91.

Iron Pier

33. Congress Street to Windsor Street on Beach Drive. Original site of the Windsor Hotel which succumbed to fire in 1979. Present site is one of Cape May's condominium constructions.

Note: At this point, you may want to take a slight detour from the auto tour route and continue to the end of Beach Drive where you will see a lovely seaside view of Cape May Point and Lighthouse. If the timing is right, you'll be treated to a sunset over the ocean.

> *To continue tour: Turn right on Broadway (North Rt. 626).*

34. 8 Broadway, *Wilmon Willdin Florida Cottage*, 1883 (private residence): Moved to this site from Cold Spring Village in 1900. Lovely example of the Bungalow Style house. Note intricate hooded dormer windows, acroteria, classic porch posts and original picket fence.

35. 416 Broadway, *The Fow House*. Built in 1690's, the rear section of this historic farmhouse was originally a whaler's cottage. The front part was added in 1874.

> *Make a left turn at the stop light onto Sunset Boulevard (606W).*

36. 1 Sunset Boulevard, West Cape May **(Peaches at Sunset).** Innovative restoration of a vintage private home for an alternative use. Restaurant. Seasonal.

37. Junction 606 and corner So. Bayshore Road (Rt. 607) **(South Meadow Cottage).** This tiny pink cottage was once the top floor of a two story house! The hurricane of 1962 destroyed the entire lower portion of the house. Across the street to your left is a migratory bird refuge, wetlands and finally the beach.

AUTO TOUR
LOOP B: SITES 38-58

LOOP B: CAPE MAY POINT

Pass sign for Junction 629 to reach Junction 651 and Cape May Point. Make a left, driving between the cement pillars onto Cape May Avenue. This is the entranceway to Cape May Point. Originally the town of Sea Grove, it was developed as a religious retreat and summer resort for members of the Presbyterian Church. Lake Lily is to your left.

Continue on Cape Avenue, riding toward the blinking sign at the circle ahead. Just before the sign, note the church on your right and pull over. This is a good spot to stop and read the History of Cape May Point and to look over the tour map on the next two pages. Loop B Sites begin on page 85.

Lighthouse at Cape May Point.

History of Cape May Point
(Sea Grove)

In 1874, the small community of Sea Grove was planned nearer to the steamboat landing at Cape May Point. The town as originally developed as a religious retreat and a summer resort for members of the Presbyterian Church. It was one of a number of similar Protestant communities that were constructed in the 1870's. (The Monmouth County, New Jersey shore resort of Ocean Grove, founded by the Methodists, was perhaps the most famous of these.) The layout of Sea Grove was carefully planned—at the very center of the community, a circular plot was set aside for the location of an open pavilion for religious services. Radiating from the religious center, broad avenues were laid out with residential streets in between. The oceanfront was set aside for mansions and summer hotels. The plan was to create a pleasing compromise between religious pursuits and commercial development. Despite the attractive plans, Sea Grove never grew beyond its earliest boundaries and at its height it had fewer than one hundred buildings.

Opposite page, top: Rustic Gate to Sea Grove. Bottom: Lake Lily. Above, top to bottom: The Pavilion; Bird's Eye View of Sea Grove; Original Lighthouse at Cape May Point. Illustrations are reproductions of original etchings.

Daveys
Lake

POND CREEK

Bay

BEACH

SUNSET

Delaware

SUNSET BOULEVARD

Lighthouse Ave

Lake Drive

Alexander Ave

Cedar Ave

Lake
Lily

Holly Ave

Lake Ave

Knox Ave

Ocean

Cape Ave.

Dr

Stites Ave

38

Brainard

Oxford

48

Chrystal Ave

Central

Pavilion
39
Ave.

Cambridge

Pearl

Princeton

Av
40

Yale

Ave

41

Lincoln

Ave

42

43

CAPE
MAY
POINT

H

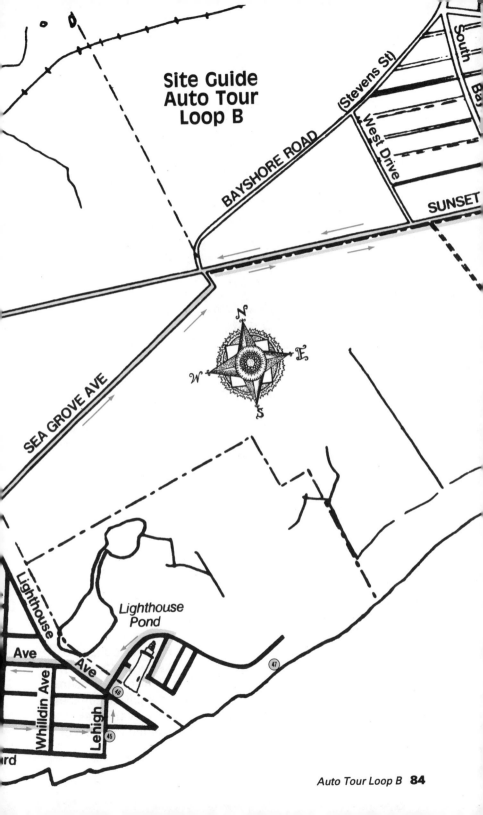

Site Guide
Auto Tour
Loop B

BAYSHORE ROAD (Stevens St)

West Drive

South Bay

SUNSET

SEA GROVE AVE

N W E S

Lighthouse Ave

Lighthouse Pond

Ave

Whilldin Ave

Lehigh

46

47

45

Beadle Memorial Presbyterian Church.　　　　　　*M. Cudworth*

38. Cape Avenue, **Beadle Memorial Presbyterian Church**, 1882: Similar in symmetrical design to the Cape Island Presbyterian Church on Decatur Street in Cape May. Note the use of more modest building materials and a combination of popular architectural styles–Gothic windows, Stick-style trim and Queen Anne mixed building textures.

> *Drive around circle until you reach the continuation of Cape Avenue (2nd right) and turn right.*

39. The Circle **(Pavilion Avenue)**: The very center of town, midway between the ocean and Cape Island Road (Sunset Boulevard)–this plot of land was the location of a towered octagonal pavilion reserved for religious purposes. (See historical drawing on previous page.)

40. 301 Cape Avenue and corner of Yale Avenue, *Cottage of John Wanamaker* **(Marianist Family Retreat Center)**: During the summers of 1890-91, President Benjamin Harrison and his wife spent much of their time here at the private cottage owned by his Postmaster General, John Wanamaker. Wanamaker was a militant Protestant and one of the founders of Sea Grove.

Diagonally across the street view:

41. S.E. corner Cape and Yale Avenues, *The Croll-Blackburn House*, ca. 1872. Magnificently restored private residence notable for many classic characteristics of the Carpenter Gothic Revival style. Notice the variety of fancy wooden jig-saw details (bargeboard, brackets and spandrels), pointed, hooded windows topped with carved finials; unusual clustered columns. Lovely views of dunes and ocean.

> *To continue the tour, follow curve in road to your left. (Cape Avenue changes to Lincoln).*

NOTE: This area abounds with natural beauty. It seems as if time has stool still ... narrow winding roads along the beach, tall dunes and grasses, if possible, park your car and climb the wooden plants over the dunes to the beach and take a stroll.

42. Numbers 415 to 404: Early Cape May Point cottages.

Turn right onto Ocean Avenue.

M. Cudworth

St. Peter's by the Sea

43. Corner Ocean Avenue and Lake Drive. **St. Peter's by the Sea**, 1876: A charming example of a small structure with Stick-style ornamentation over vertical tongue and groove siding. It is believed that this building was originally built for the Centennial Expo of 1876 in Philadelphia and later moved to the Point.

> *Go around St. Peter's making a sharp left onto Lake Drive. Go one block to Lincoln and make a right.*

44. 301 Lincoln (corner Coral on left). Notable triple pointed Gothic windows and tower at rear of house. Private residence.

Note mix of old and newly restored private homes in this area. Continue to corner and make a right on Lincoln. As you cross over Coral, a glimpse of the lighthouse will be on your left. Cross over Whilden Avenue, continue to corner of Lehigh; on right view:

45. Corner Lincoln and Lehigh, **St. Mary's by the Sea**: In 1913, this building, the Shoreham Hotel, was sold to the Sisters of the Convent of the Sacred Heart and turned into a summer retreat.

Turn left at Lehigh, facing the Lighthouse and Cape May Point Municipal Building. Continue on Lehigh crossing over Yale Avenue to enter Cape May Point State Park (43). This is a good place to stop and rest. Follow signs for parking.

46. Lighthouse and Cape May Point State Park: This 165 foot lighthouse is one of the County's oldest landmarks and is the third recorded lighthouse at the Point. It is reportedly the oldest lighthouse that is still U.S. Coast Guard commissioned as a navigational aid. The brick structure was started in 1857 and first lit on October 31, 1859 and originally powered by sperm whale oil! Exterior walls are 3'9" of solid brick at the base and the interior contains a cast-iron spiral staircase leading to the watchroom gallery. The 199-step tower is open to the public with admission fee. Ongoing restoration efforts include a new paint job in the original colors, a totally reconstructed lantern and a Visitors' Orientation Center and museum shop in the adjacent Oil House. Admission to the orientation center and ground floor of the lighthouse is free. Cape May Point State Park also has a Nature Center and is a haven for bird-watchers with its sanctuary, walking trails and elevated lookout pavilion. On the beach is a World War II concrete bunker **(47)** which is no longer accessible to the public due to severe coastal erosion.

*Upon leaving the Park area, return to the entrance street (Lehigh) by following the exit signs. Make a sharp right onto Lighthouse Avenue. Go one block to Whilden Avenue and make a left, then a very quick right onto Princeton. Go two blocks to Lake Drive and make a right. Drive two blocks to Lily Lake **(48)** and bear to the right of* *the lake. Pass Oxford Street (first right), slow down, park and settle down on a park bench to feed the swans and other water fowl or to watch the lovely sunset!*

To return to Cape May proper, make a right on Sea Grove Avenue just ahead, and follow the road past wooded areas, seaside farms and several historic private properties. At the stop light at Broadway, you will notice a narrow park ahead on your left. On the far side of the park is a large red and tan house.

Use Auto Tour Loop A map (map p.65) for Sites 49-58. Follow broken line route.

49. 133 Myrtle Avenue, (overlooking Wilbraham Park), **(Wilbraham Mansion and Inn)**, 1840: Originally a farmhouse built by Judith Hughes, a Mayflower descendant. In 1900, the property was acquired by J. W. Wilbraham, a wealthy Philadelphia industrialist who made the interior and exterior "Victorian renovations". Notice the iron fence around the estate, made in John Wilbraham's foundry. Today, the mansion is operated as a Bed & Breakfast Inn with an indoor pool. Open all year.

Bernard Good House.   M. Cudworth H. Michaels

Continue on West Perry Street, bearing left at the stop light. Look for the purple house on the right:

50. 238 Perry Street (on right, just after the light), **The Barnard-Good House**, 1868: Early Second Empire mansard cottage built on property which was part of the original Congress Hall estate. Notice wealth of "gingerbread" trim, turned-wood porch columns, wrap-around porch and lovely picket fence bordering house and gardens. Bed & Breakfast Inn. Seasonal.

After passing light, bear to left side of parking lot ahead (Jackson Street). Go one block to Lafayette Street and make a sharp left around the small triangle in road.

Cape May Community Information Center. (HABS)

*On your left as you turn, view the historic buildings today housing **All Irish Imports**, and the **Cape May Community Information Center**.*

51. 417 Lafayette Street, *Cape Island Presbyterian Church*, 1853 **(Cape May Community Information Center)**: This structure replaced the "Visitors' Church" which stood on Washington Street in 1844. The formal facade is enriched with classic detailing of the Georgian Revival style. The building is a rare example of the Exotic Revival style displaying Moorish influence on the onion shaped dome and the horseshoe arches of the cupola. These "exotic" styles became known to Americans through French and British expeditions in the East.

You may wish to end your tour here at the Information Center. (Parking lot on left.)

52. All Irish Imports (next to Information Center), 1879: This tiny building formerly stood on Beach and Guerney Streets as part of the old Stockton Hotel. This 19th century beachfront bathhouse is the only building which survived from the highly elaborate Stockton complex.

Cape Island Baptist Church. (HABS)

> NOTE: There are many more historical sites on Lafayette Street which was one of the two earliest (1833) public roads laid out in Cape Island (the other early street was Perry). Do continue down this still heavy traveled street noting these significant structures:

53. 727-731 Franklin Street (corner Lafayette), *Cape Island Baptist Church* **(Franklin Street United Methodist Church)**, 1879: Elaborately styled parish Gothic design.

54. Corner Lafayette and Jefferson Streets, *Samuel Marcy House*, (private residence): 18th century all brick house with single gable roof. Originally the "Plantation House" of Dr. Samuel Marcy, who built a large hotel called "Whitehall" which stood adjacent to this property.

55. 1023-1035 Lafayette Street, the old *Cape May Golf Clubhouse*, ca. 1870.

56. 1037 Lafayette Street, *William Townsend House*, 1833 (private residence).

57. 1142 Lafayette Street, *Daniel Ware House,* (private residence): Built in 1846 and has remained in the family of the original owner.

Josiah Schellinger House (The Octagonal House).   M. Cudworth

58. 1286-1288 Lafayette Street, *Josiah Schellinger House,* **(The Octagonal House)** 1875, (private residence).

> *To reach this Exotic Revival structure at the very end of Lafayette, you must go around this "one way" block—make a right on Sidney Street, a left on Washington Street, bear left at the triangle, left at gas station and another left at the Cape May Marlin & Tuna Club to get back onto Lafayette Street. Go slow at this point—the Octagonal House will be seen immediately upon turning this corner.*

The Octagonal style was developed and popularized in 1848 by Orson Squire Fowler with the publication of his book, *"A Home for All or the Gravel Wall and the Octagon Mode of Building".* Fowler considered the octagon to be the ideal plan for domestic architecture—20% larger than a square house of the same perimeter, with more light and earlier to heat and cool. This is the only example in Cape May and fits well into the Exotic Revival style which enjoyed an abbreviated period of popularity in the 19th Century.

Acknowledgements

First and foremost, the deepest thanks go to all the citizens of Cape May, the custodians of one of the largest collections of late 19th Century frame buildings left in the U.S. today.

For sharing their expertise and wealth of historical knowledge, many thanks go to the individuals who provide the extremely entertaining Guided Tours sponsored by Mid-Atlantic Center of the Arts (MAC).

The following books and publications have been particularly helpful in preparing this historical information and architectural details appearing in this guidebook. They are highly recommended to you for further reading.

Alexander, Robert Crozer. *Ho! For Cape Island*, Cape May, NJ: 1956.

Blumenson, John J.G. *Identifying American Architecture*, New York, NY: W.W. Norton & Co., Inc., 1977.

Cape Island Historical Celebration Committee. *The Historical Diary of Cape Island.* Cape May, NJ: 1964.

McAlester, Virginia and Lee. *A Field Guide To American Houses.* New York, NY: Alfred A. Knopk, 1984.

Pitts, Carolyn; Fish, Michael; McCauley, Hugh J.; Vauk, Trina. *The Cape May Handbook.* Philadelphia, PA: The Athenaeum of Philadelphia, 1977.

Thomas, George and Doebley, Carl. Cape May, *Queen of the Seaside Resorts.* Cranbury, NJ: Associated University Presses, Inc., 1977.

The History of Cape May was reproduced from *Victorian Holidays*, New York, NY: Lady Raspberry Press, 1982. (Marsha Cudworth and Howard Michaels, authors).

Further appreciation goes to the Mid-Atlantic Center for the Arts (MAC), for the use of historical illustrations from the Physick Estate Library. The composite of old etchings of Sea Grove (Cape May Point) was reprinted from Scheyichbi and the Strand (1876).

Historic American Building Survey (HABS) drawings were done by the Cape May Survey Teams of 1973, 1974, and 1977. Carolyn Pitts–Director; Hugh McCauley–Chief Architect. HABS drawings appearing in this publication prepared by Perry Benson, Gardener Cadwalader, Dan B. Goodenow, Thomas Ewing, H. Reed Longnecker, Hugh McCauley and Daniel McCoubrey. This survey supervised the measuring, drawing, researching and recording of Cape May's historic structures. Documentation is deposited in the Library of Congress, Washington, D.C.